A GOLD MINE

A GOLD MINE

A Collection of Poetry
by Dale Brabb

LUMINARE PRESS
WWW.LUMINAREPRESS.COM

A Gold Mine: A Collection of Poetry
Copyright © 2021 by Dale Brabb

All rights reserved. This book or any portion thereof may not be reproduced or used in any manner whatsoever without the express written permission of the publisher, except for the use of brief quotations in a book review.

Printed in the United States of America

Cover Art by Michael Kelly

Luminare Press
442 Charnelton St.
Eugene, OR 97401
www.luminarepress.com

LCCN: 2021915438
ISBN: 978-1-64388-768-5

*I dedicate this book of poetry to
my children and theirs.*

*It is full of nuggets, this gold mine,
and I hope they will be enriched by them.*

Table of Contents

Chapter One
Family Trees 1

Chapter Two
War in Our Time 23

Chapter Three
The Passage of Time 45

Chapter Four
A Many Splendored Thing 75

Chapter Five
The Natural World 113

Chapter Six
Odd Grandpa 135

Chapter Seven
The Funny Papers 189

About the Author 217

Chapter One

FAMILY TREES

*My family has had a big influence
on my poetry.*

Wild Horses in Utah

She left me to go ride wild horses in Utah
her and the baby we didn't know she carried
breaking Spanish mustangs on some ranch

The boy in the picture looks relieved
having put her on a bus at the border
glad to be shut of her to be honest
now it was just him and the dog
she left behind

I remember that feeling of freedom
basking in ignorance to a fault
while history was being made
one cell division at a time

On the way back south
we camped in the Cimarron Canyon
laughing and splashing
high on acid
and failing to dam the creek
even for a little while

Tiny Pieces of the heart

A tiny heart beating in a tiny breast
pieces of my own heart divided
in a girl named Jazmin
my baby's baby born

And just the night before
I dreamt my father sat down beside me smiling
he didn't interrupt
just sat there like he knew something
which I'd find out by and by

I was once a tiny piece of his heart
my daughter named for his mother
and now this baby Jazmin girl
my first grand-daughter

She will never know my father
or her mother's namesake
but who left with her a gift anyway
she can't help but pass along
in tiny pieces of the heart

Through the Veils

She was too empathetic
her house a kitty Lost and Found
the sick ones she'd nurse
and heart broken when the nursing failed
she'd bring them their bodies to me

And I would take the box from her
(for she could never bear
to see what death obscured)
through veils of her falling tears
I'd bury another one in my yard

This time it's not the same
it's her husband dying now
a man I once called friend
I can not help her bear it
no one can

We learn or we don't
either we see through dirt
raining down on the box
or we close our eyes
neither changes the outcome

Strings

We are connected to the world with strings
hanging from our family trees
society's macramé
political marionettes
religious webs

Every parent cries
when the cords are cut
for as much as we seek connection
we abhor separation
yet it must be

Our strings serrated we must begin
a new tapestry
tying knots temporarily
few of us with a plan
until the worms get in
so tenuous our silken life

Fragile strings of family
like rubber bands pulled too far
reel in the line
and you're gifted with what was
until pulling in the yet on the end of the line

We are but strings fraying
a woven fabric
someone in the future could study
if knots we've tied
will stand the test of time
or just be hay for moths

The Pepper

My cousin slipped a hot pepper
into the jar of sweet pickles
she gave me years before she died
I just found it
like a message in a bottle
totally at odds
with Grandma's German recipe
which is why I loved her so
and when the pickles are finally gone
I'll have that pepper to remember

The Lord's Prayer

Mom asked me to sing The Lord's Prayer
to a church full of people
at Dad's funeral
it would mean so much to him

She always asked me to sing
trotting me out like a dancing bear
to perform for the public
I could do what she couldn't

But that day grief dissolved my face
words were washed away
like I was drowning
and I couldn't sing

Maybe sometime I'll sing it for them again
now there's no hurry
and no one left to watch a weeping bear
stumble through his lonely dance

Solace

I used to bake bread for my family
when I was first married
using the Tassajara bread-book
stained now from usage
there was a solace I found in kneading

On Sundays I'd roast some beef too
like my mother had always done
and so I had wonderful sandwiches to eat
each day at college
working my way to a different future
and learning to fend for myself
lessons I would recommend to anyone
if for no other reason
than to enjoy the solace found in kneading

Nothing ever works out the way you thought it would
and it doesn't really matter in the long run
but the skills I've learned to survive
allow me to be this frank
and though stained now from usage
I am not immune to solace

Side Streets

I had not planned on those side streets
leading away from home
when what was familiar changed
in this dream we call reality

I have a nice apartment
high ceilings for my lofty thoughts
the dust of other people's past
mixing with my own fresh

I planted roses around the holly tree
pruning them like Grandma Mae taught me
and if I'd lived somewhere else
I would have done the same

The native peoples of this place
had different homes in different seasons
but the fire-ring remained the same
to know thyself recognize your ashes

Sedimentary Rocks

In his eighties my father told me
he still felt like his sixteen year old self
was looking through his old eyes
and wondering how all this happened
how he only got older
on the outside
while inside we remain youthful

While our now ran to then
we were not paying attention
focused on details of the day
and the years added up
like sedimentary rock built layer on layer
and we've got to consciously shrug some of it off
like fossils must do
just to be visible anymore

Rescue Blueberries

My blueberries are covered with blossoms
when I got them they were banzai
refugees abandoned
to a repressive regime
sheltered next to a shed
lucky if they got any sun
all around them doused with Roundup

They are emigrants to me
transplanted to my soil
rescue blueberries
and now my family
adding sweetness to my life
see that wasn't so hard

Measuring up

Life is a process of building trail
and when the stones are put down
something like a path results
both meandering and straight
maybe it goes where you meant it to
but there are no rules to measure it

The child is free to walk away
a gift not yours to keep
cords untied
an untethered piece of soul
set free without expectation of return
though you never cease to want to hear
familiar footsteps
there is no rule to measure them

Love is a vessel without a brim
you may not see its surface
it is not a mirror for your reflection
deep or shallow
but when it's full spills right over
satisfying unknown thirsts
without measure

I stood and toasted you my daughter
crediting your mother for your success
as a complete and wonderful person
but when you whispered
"You are the best dad I could have had"
an inner smile spread all over my face
because even without any rules
followed or broken
I'd still measured up

Potluck in Heaven

My cousin left me a jar of pickled beets
may she rest in peace
no doubt she put them up herself
on one of those hot afternoons in Idaho
an old family recipe I'm sure
she knew I would appreciate

She never gave much credence
to Biblical myths
but were there to be a potluck in heaven
(every Sunday)
down by the River Jordan
alongside the fried chicken
and potato salad
would be an eternal bowl
(in accordance with our heritage)
of my cousin's pickled beets

Making sense of history

When I was ten I had an operation for hernia
so of course they put me under
coming out of the anesthesia I had a dream
of being underwater and drowning
the surface beckoned
I struggled to reach it
but just as I got there
something thrust me down to start again
over and over again it happened

Speaking to my father many years later
he told me of his role that day
I kept trying to sit up
and mindful of my fresh stitches
he pressed me back down for safety's sake
suddenly it all made sense
one memory out of many
brought to me in technicolor

I couldn't help but hug the old man
love had made him do it
and how was I to fault that?

CHUTNEY BOY

Far under the shed he's gone
in the murky light
I see his dim form and refuge
the family's dog

I talk to him as I crawl
under the beams
telling him what a fine dog he is
but I feel he is ashamed
to be too sick to come to me

I cradle his head
whispering love into his velvet ear
a tail tries a feeble wag
we begin our journey toward the light

It is no coincidence
that my heart breaks twice
for Chutney was just a puppy
when my wife and I were new
and now divorce and death
mark the length of one dog's life
and all retrieving past

Dale Brabb

I brush the dirt and leaves
off his golden hide
and take him gently in my arms
for a short trip in the car
which he used to enjoy

He lays very still
while medicines of mercy are prepared
my now ex-wife and I
avoiding eye contact across the sterile table
and feeling very much alone
I tell him as the needle finds its mark
good bye my Chutney Boy

Grandpa

Squatting in the dusty barn
I listened as the old men talked
while blue smoke shafted in the sun
the heavy smell of tractor oil
would take me back again

Grandpa took a shine to me
I thought we all just looked the same
he never had much time for kids
but I had maybe something else
we could see it in each other's eyes
the eyes of the carpenter

And at the cabin he had built
the Big Wood running close beside
we waded through the rapids there
hoping for some breakfast trout
while the others lay asleep

When I saw you lying there
a waxy glow past living's grip
and heard that mason droning on
I was unashamed of my own tears
a grandpa I had lost
but the tears were for my friend

Beautiful children

It's hard for some people to understand
that there is only one race
the race of humans
not now nor ever will we achieve racial purity
except to accept we're all racially pure
check the DNA
it is irrefutable

My father was in Brazil during WWII
a member of the American military
he told me of a country he had seen
of mixed blacks and whites
and of the beautiful children
running through the streets
every shade of color
it made me hope to fit in
to the inexorable future

Passing the ball

I remember my grandchildren
chasing me down the yard
sunhat and feet flapping
and me with the ball at my feet
there is even a picture of it
those were the days

They could catch me easy now
in spite of all my old age and trickery
and take the ball off my feet
running away faster
than I can ever catch them
which is only just
as it was their ball we were playing with all along

Chapter Two

WAR IN OUR TIME

There are many forms that war takes

A SOLDIER DIED FOR YOU TODAY

A soldier died for you today
a bomb planted by the side of the road
cut his dreams
his family
our future
short

He died for your freedom say our leaders
in some other country
he died for you
say our leaders

A soldier died for you today
called an 'occupier'
in a language he didn't understand
dying for your freedom
in some other country

He died for our country
for all the flag-waving children
for all the decorated men
marching in parades
for all the heartfelt thanks
he died for you

A soldier died for you today
occupying some other country
how many more must die
before we're finally free

Altered gods

Yet again with fear-filled eyes the people turned and ran
the towers burned and crushed a nation's innocence
    that day
for hate still rules the heart of modern man

With a shaky hand a president endorsed an angry plan
and when a toadstool cloud had doomed those islands
    far away
yet again with fear-filled eyes the people turned and ran

A country averted its shameful face and failed to take
    a stand
when smoke from burning bodies turned blue sky
    ugly gray
for hate still rules the heart of modern man

Flowered girls smiled at solemn soldiers before rioting
    began
but the order came and shots rang out to keep the
    crowd at bay
yet again with fear-filled eyes the people turned and ran

Jealousy and vengeance coursed across an ancient land
cruelty and ethnic cleansing the tyrant's path
for hate still rules the heart of modern man

Modern men still pile the dead in Death's bloody hands
science invents new ways to kill and to altered gods
    they pray
yet again with fear-filled eyes the people turned and ran
for hate still rules the heart of modern man

Around the corner

I never knew your name
passing as we did in the night
you standing crouched
a six-foot scrap of metal
clenched in your fists like a spear
under a street-light you stood
your shadow cast on the wall
where narrow streets converged

You were a Marine
I could tell it from your haircut
part of the Third Division
newly pulled out of Nam
civilian clothes looking strange
in a military stance
you stared at something I couldn't see
breath hissing through your teeth
all this seen suddenly
as I stepped around the corner

I was heading through the village
up the hill to my apartment
my mind reeling on LSD
(I'd just come from a nightclub
called the Fillmore East
the light show and amped-up music
had been too much to take
and the attempt to connect to my culture

just left me feeling foreign)
in the darkness surrounding me
the air was buzzing with color
and then I turned the corner
where you were hiding in the light

Somehow I knew not to make eye contact
as if doing so would surely draw me into war
you looked threatened by unseen enemies
and I was way too real
entering your perilous personal space
I looked up the street past you
and willed my feet to walk on normally
and so I went right by
like you weren't even there

I wonder where you are today
and if you have bad dreams
of when you were so frightened
still caught up in a jungle
where there was no safe place to be
and though I didn't have to go
I never will forget
the night you brought Vietnam to me

Footprints on the Moon

I spent almost two years at Onna Point on Okinawa
last I heard it was all gone
the antenna field clear-cut to grow pineapples
our top-secret compound secreted away
but it's still filed in my memory

Especially the NCO club
and its slot machines
I remember one morning
just got off night shift
three quarters in my pocket
I got two cherries and won six more
and then hit a thirty-five dollar jackpot
which I had to stand guard over
since it didn't pay off in coins
and too early for the manager

So I leaned against the machine
and watched a TV mounted up in the corner
a grainy black and white picture
of a space-man stepping down
onto a dusty surface

Dale Brabb

And then him saying something about
giant steps and mankind
and leaving footprints on the moon
for all eternity to see
and I got to watch it happen live on TV
with such hope for mankind's future

I probably should have been more impressed
in retrospect
but at the time
I was envisioning going downtown
and thirty-five dollars I hadn't even got yet
already burning live holes in my pocket

Independence Day

Tonight the country celebrates
its perennial war of independence
acted out in every street
strings of crackers going off
like automatic weapons
bombshells bursting overhead
like in the National Anthem

The thought occurs to me
perhaps I'm not an American after all
looking sidewise at the dogs and cats
under the bed with me
hiding from freedom's frightening display

Lucy in the sky

Driving home up the coast road
that time on Okinawa fifty years ago
looking west over the South China Sea
a twisty and turning road it was
coral lagoons below flooded with the tide
and a full moon's light
riding in a convertible

The driver was a surfer
on loan to the military from California
a rich kid with a convertible
but since we were down to seeds and stems
we'd eaten acid
and so he fell in love with the moon

Well it was right there
how could you not fall in love with it?
except he was also driving the car
on a road I wish he'd look at sometimes
twisty and turning as it was
above those moonlit lagoons

It makes me wonder to this day
how I ever got home safe

Quality

There is no quality or quantity to "truth"
a thing isn't more "truthful" because it has more truth in it
either it is true or it is not

There is no quality to "lies"
a thing does not approach truth if it is a lie
others may qualify "lies" as they wish
but I say either it is the truth or it is a lie

If you would choose lies over truth
then I hope you never get a position
of leadership
because you clearly lack the quality

Refugees

It makes me sad when foreign policy
devolves into a pissing contest
when the national hard-on
motivates our national penis
and we rape and pillage
to the will of profiteers
the killing of people
and destruction of their homes
just collateral damage
as we defend our freedom

We have learned this lesson well
taking over from our British founders
and now the sun never sets
on the Star Spangled Banner

People don't hate us for our freedom
they hate us because we deny them theirs
if we weren't so busy being privileged
in this latest age
we'd see ourselves again
as the refugees we were
back in our beginnings
back when the future blinded us to hindsight

Semper fi

Vietnam snared you like a spider my brother
and now you are an old bug
wrapped in a web of memory
both victim and predator
you came home a hollow tattooed shell

You are sad my brother
because you did not die on the killing fields
but lived to watch your brothers murder themselves
with nightmares
with guns and bad drugs

No one celebrated your return my brother
no photos of flags on nameless hills to revere
and the shreds of honor you earned
stretch across the decades like an old scar

You still clutch your worn-out hatreds my brother
like they were medals
and no one in this changed world
wants to share them
so you stand in the Vet's club
a bottle in your hand
shouting at the other drunks
"Semper fi"
like an angry benediction

It is so sad my brother
you've been always faithful unto death
and let life pass you by

Semper fi my brother
Semper fi

The door-knocker

It was a red-headed woodpecker
that when you pulled the cord hanging down
there was no doubt you had knocked
the sound penetrating through my apartment

A former lover had given it to me
and this folk-art had graced my front door
for twenty years

My upstairs neighbor quit taking her meds
my first clue being the skull and crossbones
drawn on my door-jamb
I scrubbed it out

But I was troubled by it
was I poison or a pirate?
and after almost a year of peace
since her last episode of insanity

She is a gardener
I'd filled the yard with raised beds long before she arrived
and in a letter to defuse what poison she felt from me
I retired from gardening and gave it all to her
when she read it she went beserk

Dale Brabb

Did I mention she was off her meds?
she began to break things
first she broke things upstairs in her apartment
maybe she was trying to break my letter

Then I heard this tremendous hammering on my door
and when I opened it she was threatening me
with her stave like she knew how to use it
on the door was written "your dead"

That time she backed off and just told me to kill myself
"You're old and dead"
and such like

But she came back with her stick
and knocked my woodpecker from its perch
took it with her I guess
I doubt I'll see it again
A friend has offered me a replacement knocker
which is tempting
but I don't think it would do to mount it now
with times being so uncertain

Shoot the guns

In my country there are more guns than people
and the guns are killing us
they are shooting us down
in schools
in public places
in houses of worship
the list goes on and on

Kill the guns
before they kill more people
it won't be easy
the guns look after their kind
they have friends in high places
and have allied with money

But we must shoot the guns
kill them with their own peers if must be
and then melt them down
until we outnumber them again

Dale Brabb

The Fear of Others

I am an other to you
you are an other to me
love one another
just words in a book

Others closing eyes to sleep
dream of other things
their normal as alien to us
as our usual is strange to them

I have seen the others
and they are not like us
they are us
jumped down from the same family trees
and fighting reunion nail and claw

Every altar bloodied
by repulsion too attractive to resist
no weapon invented can defend us
from the fear of others

Your bullet

I am your bullet
hand-loaded in a magazine
or mass-produced in a ribbon of destruction
fired at random I took you by chance
or in the cross-hairs
your name was all over me
I get no medals
though I produce tears
no matter where I do my job
I'm not heroic

I am your bullet
I could have missed you
I could have bounced off a wall
or your body-armor
but I didn't
I have no concern for your future cut short
and the children you'll never have
or those left behind with your grieving widow
because I don't care about your family
I don't care about your picture shown in silence
as your name is made available

Dale Brabb

I am your bullet
and I will not stop killing
until weapons stop firing me
I don't need flags and patriotism
prayers or pretty speeches
all I need is a finger to send me
on an order issued by someone far away
or in a spasm of hate right here at home
I am not designed to know right from wrong
I'm just a bullet and you are a target
it is really that simple

I am your bullet
and I am not guilty of anything
nor should I be
I am just doing a job
the job you manufactured me to do
if there is a flaw in my design
look in a mirror to see it

We bought rockets

A pandemic has surfaced
in my lifetime
and I am prime beef for it

Day two of isolation
not much has changed
drove my car on empty streets

We bought so many rockets
you'd think I would feel safe
but this is a different kind of war

Chapter Three

THE PASSAGE OF TIME

*In this chapter are poems dealing with various aspects
of time, including life expectancy, eternity, our
conception of time, and of course,
the passage of time.*

A poetic image

Not even a week into September
I saw the first casualty
skittering down the street
a maple-leaf dried to the bone
making noise clicking along the pavement
like a tap-dancer

Quite a poetic image
to leave a noise
that might be heard
as you skip on out of here

April at Anan

In the morning I carry my coffee down the boardwalk
to the little bay
where the stream empties into the ocean
a place few people have seen
or ever see

The tide doesn't sleep there
and I sit with my back to a mossy rock
sipping coffee and smoking
around the corner is a tidal lagoon
now full
now empty
each morning different in its sameness.

A mink scurries under a rock
on which a young eagle lands
a split second too late for breakfast
crab shells from our dinner
are visible at the low tide
across the way ducks by the dozens
squabble in the shallows
and under a root-wad a bear's stomach growls
dreaming of skunk cabbage and fresh grass
the taste of leaping silver fish

And I know how lucky I am to be here
across the bay snow-covered mountains
whales booming like cannons in the sound
otters on a rock loudly eating a crab
my eyes the only difference
and when I'm gone
all will be as before

Decaying orbit

A warm snap in Winter
makes me almost giddy
like a tree with the sap rising
or a bulb about to kick up its heels
we are attuned without knowing
our mortality built in
making hay if the sun will but shine

Nobody knows their "sell on date"
warranties were not issued for our model
and like some satellite launched long ago
a message in a bottle
we wake now and again
sending signals from our decaying orbit
hoping somebody somewhere gets them
before it's all too late

Dreams of flying

"To live is so startling it leaves little
time for anything else"
EMILY DICKINSON

Think of what it takes to live
just maintaining the machinery of the body
wears one out
yet the soul dreams effortlessly of flying

To the child's senses life is so startling
the young body flying headlong
in pursuit of everything
until laid down almost unaware by dreaming sleep

We grow up to work leaving few moments
to chase youthful dreams
years leap by while we trudge along
new experiences submerging memory

Finally we're left with little time
a commodity we cannot replenish
and yet the timeless soul of a child looks out
from wrinkled eyes

Duty has left our bodies too tired for anything else
but a well-deserved nap on the porch
so practice soaring there
until everything flies away

Estimated Time of Departure

I knew she'd gotten worse
I'd heard reports of her decline
at Thanksgiving she'd been capable
of being there
and now no telling
where she was

She searched my face
with a blank intensity
and finally smiled a little smile
"I recognize you"
she told me
"and I recognize you" I said
giving her a hug

I remember her as a laughing lively girl
skiing down the mountain-side headlong
me barely keeping up
but that was long ago
and now I see that same face
taken by senility
those same lips that kissed me
searching for names to put to faces

I am both sad and gladdened
thinking back
because perhaps that laughing girl inside
saw me one last time
smiling at me and waving
like from a window on an airplane
that took off too soon

Expectations

Dark and dank the stones smoothly
scored by finger-nailed generations
mute resistance to a seeming fate
the residue of days uncounted
mortared and sealed
the mason's touch
my own ancient mold
depressing me beneath its weight

The church's cornerstone was set by sins
without them there would be no wall
no cloistered recollections where
deeply sought deliverance
falls short before the gaze of God
and fingers trace recanted beads
clothed in habits by the saints
guttered flame the only light

The mother and the father both
to protect against the world outside
safe within these walls succor
with battering words and welting belt
all for the best they thought to build
until both curious and unprepared
and with map-less freedom thrust naïve
a child then takes first halting steps
into this unforgiving maze we call society

And laws provide imprisonment
encase the libraries thick with Latin spells
black-robed vultures feed upon
the carcass of recalcitrance
and if you walk that narrow path
you'll live to see another day
just like the last in unseen subtle chains
the greater good controls the course
a blinded bar no peers can cross

With all these stones I've built my cell
I hear your voice call from beyond
in guilt and expiation I reside
until with my egg-tooth can break free
this rocky shell dismantles piece by piece
fragments firmly put aside
I am divine
I am a deconstructed myth
a broken link of history
and in this sunny warmth of now
shake out my wings to dry

Earning perspective

I had old eyes early
like Sasquatch on TV a friend said
dogs always take to me

My eyes have grown no younger
though so many things they observe
remind me of my youth
seen through reading glasses

I have become a beholder
with these old eyes
every now a new past tense
as I earn perspective

Eternity is now

I let all my watches run down
and tossed out the calendar too
yet time will on
measured or no

Some say time is linear
but I say it is pervasive
history and predictions are full of it
like that is reality
when all we really know is now

We take a chance every time we sleep
and relinquish our present
true faith is believing we'll wake up
for time will stop forever
that first time we don't

Follow me

So far time has been linear for me
another station always arriving
on a track extending forward and back
until I can't remember it
things irretiveable
and yet connected

So far I've been allotted a row of days
history crackling like telegraph lines
marching alongside
crossing bells echoing
without direction
only fools know where they're headed
follow me

A dirt eat dirt world

Dirt gets used up
and needs to be replenished
the raised beds show it plain
shrinking year after year
those growing plants just eat it up
and then we eat them
we eat the dirt and so it gets used up

It's simple when you think of it
as if the soil and we humans
were related in some way
maybe even taking care of each other
and how silly that sounds to say
since dirt did just fine long before
we started walking on it

But it is a dirt eat dirt world
and every shoe we wear wears out
walking on it

Losing the now

The day will surely come
when I lose the now
will I be awake or asleep?
and will I have any say
anyway?

My mother was not cognizant
on her last day
my father did not awake for his
does that limit my choices?

My neighbor used to complain
that I slammed my doors
but I think she was only jealous
because in her apartment
the doors had been removed

All these days in a line
so many nows here and gone
life marching irrevocably to a close
such is the wonder
every day facing the reality
of when I lose the now

Luck

Standing outside the bar
I was in the dark having a smoke
so I looked at the moon
to tell me where the sun was
it being important to me
to try to know where I am in the solar system
at any given moment

So much we take for granted
so long as we draw breath
so many theories
so many gods created in a relatively short time
astrologically

I was in the dark
the moon just happened to clue me in
and I felt overwhelmed with my luck
such a hoot I get to participate in existence
even with all its impermanence

Memories mine

Memories mine
because they're no one else's
or as a place to delve into
in that I've lived a long time
and mines hold history

This is an attempt to mine memories
after years of making time
rhyme with rhyme
a good student's quest
but fiction after all
and only one story I can really tell

So here we go
down the mine-shaft of memory
with a pick-axe to frighten the ghosts
and a head-lamp prone to dimming

Dale Brabb

Now

We take now for granted
of course we do
there being no way to train for it

It's easy to stack things around it
clocks and phones
trying to make our grasp of now
instantaneous

And yet we expect it somewhere else
an addendum to yesterday
(for continuance)
a tomorrow we can count on

When there is really nothing else but now
then the hardest task we have
is making sense of it
as it happens
you ready for that?

One positive aspect

One positive aspect about getting old
is that I can look at politics
and not get too upset personally

Oh I do worry for my progeny
things beyond all control
will not be better for them

So I need to take the long view
which will probably not be available to me
personally

My dream is we do better as humans
both in this world we live on
and those we share it with

I'd say wish us luck
but anything worth accomplishing
should not be left to chance

Red Horses

Red run the horses
across the canvas wall
of a cave
they leap easily
across the boundary fence

See the way they run
feet suspended indefinitely
a gallop caught forever
red bodies sculpted by the wind
and ancient pigment

A blank wall
in the cavernous darkness
but in that flash of light
I saw the horses running
they run there still

Scatter my ashes

Take me up to Cascade Head
and in resting pools
by giant moldering logs
sprinkle me among salmon smolts
and backwards let them take me out to sea
our journeys one

Then further up the trail
the creek whispers through cathedral Spruce
sift me on the gravel there
where feet will walk on top of me

When you reach the top
feed my ashes slowly
to the grasses up there
and we will dance in unison
fragile bodies fine as smoke

Then what is left
cindered bones and dust
take out along the cliff-edge
and show me to the ocean
it will send a wind to bear me up
in one final crossing of this land
back to where I started from

Dale Brabb

Sharing nows

Forever is a long time
several of them went by
since we last talked
leaving behind cobwebs
strewn with silence

I left eternity when I left church
I couldn't feel it
perhaps it hadn't got there yet
or left before I did or both
there's no way of telling

Immortality is one I know
like a thought set free now fending for itself
a memory that lost its stinger years ago
but buzzes by the ear
a spoken word echoed on the wind

But now is my most favorite word these days
I seek it every day
now is time worth sharing
and nothing is more sacred
since it's all we really have

The end of an era

It was Ralf's last night
in the restaurant he'd built from scratch
with some kind of French name
a real European chef
the first folks had seen hereabouts
a trip there an event
but now it was the end of an era
and Ralf was retiring
to play golf and swear in German

A flatbed six-pack farm pickup
pulled up along the curb
two older women got out
gussied up in their finest clothes
worn only a few times
and bought long ago
a mink coat lady
and her mother in a matching stole

It's the end of an era
the only chef they've ever known
making food with foreign names
tasting better than what they fixed at home

For us regulars at the bar
it was the end of an era too
our favorite bartender had died
behind this very bar just months before
and now Ralf was quitting
no more burger Diane made just for us

by our affable owner and chef
who only swore in German
when playing golf

The husband goes to park the truck
he'll join the women later
after taking a shot of whiskey at the bar
he's proud as he can be
wearing that suit he got for the square-dancing
back when
a perfect fit with mink coat ladies on the town

It is the end of an era
which ended long ago
the menu barely changed
except for seasonal adjustments
in twenty-five years
and no one even knew it
every time the foreign words
were new and different

Out in the bar we had our own time-warp
rehashing the same old things
except for seasonal adjustments
the usual discussion of Ralf's slice
and German Tourette's syndrome
like we thought we had forever
plainly trying to ignore
the end of an era

Silver City

It's a stack of boards now
some aligned vertically
a place dust fetches up
on the resident tumbleweeds

This isn't a city
no more than cemeteries
reflect a town's vitality
or churches overgrown by active neglect

A hundred years ago
streets muddied with commerce
ragged veins of life coursed
men and machines working day and night
an avalanche of discarded tailings
and gravestones
marking steady progress

A booming city bust
a tribute and epitaph all in one
history ignoring the present
in a crumbling clapboard ghost town
just remains of the American dream

Dale Brabb

The feather

I wake in the morning to find another feather
escaped from my pillow
how many are left?

Less future every day that passes
a pillow emptying of dreams one by one
sleep a fitting end

Memories take flight
and leave the dreamer behind
like another feather lost

The treasure

In a cove outside of Lima
dolphins chased a school of fish
right up to the sandy beach
and a silver fountain sprouted into air
flipping like coins in the sun
they leaped wanting to fly
as the dorsal fins slashed through

On the cliff a Spanish ruin
overlooks the cove
but no soldiers eye this spray of fish
and no high Inca sits in Cuzco
waiting for his share
no this time it is just me there
on an empty beach
with the treasures of the world
jumping just beyond my reach

Dale Brabb

Withered hands

Mother you seem tired
I'm not surprised
your long travail has left you spent

Your arms we took for granted
my siblings and I
looking up into your eyes
made us feel some safety
long before we'd understand
the fragility of shelter

You've sustained us all this time
though we rebelled and complained
disregarding nourishment
becoming savage get tearing at your womb
while you washed us
with loving tears

Still you try to bear us up
a thankless task
cradling an unruly brood
biting at your shrunken dugs
forgiving our unfelt guilt
yet you persist

Mother you are tired
how long before you finally let us fall
from your withered hands?

Chapter Four

A MANY SPLENDORED THING

This chapter is about love, falling in love and falling out of love.

A Box of Souvenirs

I thought you'd taken everything
when I surveyed the bare walls
and listened to the silence
where speech didn't rise
to the level of lips

Broken pieces of life
take a while to reassemble
and maybe with new attachments
but it won't look the same
besides you took the mirror
we were together in

I thought you'd taken everything
but I was wrong
you left me behind
like a box of souvenirs you no longer had use for
like a parcel left on the porch
meant to write its own forwarding address

Beyond Expiration

In my dreams she hasn't aged
though time has taken its toll
on the both of us
being now long ago divorced

In my dreams I get all the old stuff
the joys and disappointment
I've learned to live with all that
unfinished business

Dreams are a mirror I think
and she doesn't factor in my new ones
I guess memories don't age
beyond their expiration date

Chemistry

In a sea of bodies my eye is caught
ancient as a tail flicking in the forest
my blood goes up
and down with every graceful
skirt-clinging step
every ball-bearing bounce
every other thought flicked right out my head

Life is full of curiosities
we'll spend hours mulling them
debating inanities on the porch
statistics at the bar
none of it adding up to a hill of beans

When all it really takes is one tail twitch
and we'll hop down immediately
from our intellectual treetops
to scent-mark the closest fireplugs

Coyote summer

How long ago it was
making love under the stars
witnessed by an approving moon
and up on the rim-rock
coyotes sang in celebration
seemed to me

You baked pies in the wood-stove
while I sang to you
we heated rocks in the fire
and tempered our bodies
in the snow-melt creek
naked in the moonlight
we were close to gods

Somewhere the coyotes still celebrate
that old moon spying on new lovers
making moments into memories
fleet as a serenade
and yet like fossilized rock
those memories forget
how long ago it was

Dale Brabb

Diagnoses

So when I learned she'd died
of breast cancer
I was stunned

You'd think when you're lovers with someone
there would be an indelible link
a soul connection maybe
at least an upheaval of the force
palpable in its absence
but I had no idea she'd died

I realize I was the lucky one
she chose another husband than me
and he had to deal with her death
so my sadness can't compare

One time back when we were together
she made me examine her breasts
unhappy with them
since to her they were not perfect
they looked fine to me

Which just goes to show
how wrong I was
about many things
especially when it comes to relationships
and the diagnoses they inspire

Do not say that word

We are so close
breathing the same air
filling spaces with whispers
but do not say that word
you know the one
full of rings and knots and
pealing bells

Skin to skin
all silky touch
hearts and blood
passion and percussion
but do not say that word
but feel the drums

I see the sunrise on your cheek
wisdom in your silence
your scent a kind of Braille
as you finger-paint my soul
but do not say that word
don't break the spell
of this fragile web

Dale Brabb

There are so many other words to say
and perhaps when we are done with those
stories told darkness to dawn
when time has ripened like a fruit
proving beyond doubt
a truth attained

But until then
do not say that word
so we will know we mean it
when at last we do

Distant shores

I saw your footprints in the sand
there where the water takes away
those places you never walked

I thought I heard seabirds call your name
or maybe wind sculpted the sound of it
among driftwood

We've walked other beaches
our footprints crossing tides and lives
followed trails in dreams
leading to dawns and sunsets

No ancient ocean holds the answer
there is nothing not seen
but what is
catch it while you can

Duet

Looking back I think I did okay
trained by depression-era parents
I did the opposite

But I admit to a hole
an empty bucket on the list
and now there's fear I've left it too late
to ever find my dream woman

Maybe it could've made a difference
to find that someone
who could not only sing with me
but understood harmony too

Fever

We slipped out on the porch
to share a cigarette
while our respective mates
and other party-goers
stayed inside the house

We were younger
high on impossibility
hidden by the solid door we kissed
and your forbidden nipple found itself
in my trespassing hand

Later you would say to me
high up on the twelve steps program
"it was a sickness"
and then denied our love
perhaps just a rash that went away
but I was never sure

You kept your secret
I kept mine
no one ever knew but us
and though it has been many years
since that fever blazed
I still feel it in my bones

How subtle such infection is
reaching past an insubstantial door
to set me burning on a pyre of memories
stacked with relapsed regrets
as if there isn't any cure at all

Endgame

I remember a queen's bishop
slanting in again
and me a sitting duck
though most of the pressure I brought on myself
the only time I'd do anything
was to force myself

Another square beckoned
opening on a cross-road
some other queen
getting too close
and mine unconcerned
eating the apples from Eden
I was on the edge already
so of course I jumped

Fall to love

The moon came out above the rocks
we walked the cabin path
past homestead ruins
if only I had not been struck then
in those faint shadows

A wise man would have steeled his heart
against such a moon that night
against meteoric dreams
against his own frail wings
that could not break his fall to love

Getting shoes for Christmas

My wife gave me shoes one Christmas
three pair of them
gifts say it all

Oxen yoked together
start to chafe
maybe new shoes would help
take your mind off it

But even if getting shoes for Christmas
fell short of delightful
at least I was shod that year

Dale Brabb

Luring love

Love flirts around the edges
like a laughing child
bask in its delight and love may come
in time

Real love isn't to be captured
or it will chafe and change
a caged bird sings
but only songs it learned
when freedom filled its wings

We often name 'love' too soon
one piece does not finish a puzzle
until all the other parts
are found to fit

I won't be quick to say the words love
the wheel must turn
hearts and time molding
before love assumes a form

But come and play
we'll run barefoot in the grass
like laughing children
a strategy I've found successful
when it comes to luring love

Mozart after breakfast

Coffee and French toast finished
we listened to Mozart
and made love
without urgency

A special day it was
cropping up as it does in my memory now
Mozart after breakfast a rare treat
among so many moments of a life
when nothing like that had ever happened
before

Nothing lasts forever

She used a different voice as I remember
when we were seducing
I suppose I did too
not to mention hormonal sub-vocalizations
that go without saying

Those voices were constructive
and made a foundation
where they bounced around for years
until that set was finished
the whole match maybe a game
and having won nothing
we retreated with our winnings

Sticking it out for the long run
was the course abandoned
after all it hadn't worked in the past
even when put up on a pedestal
nothing lasts forever
with memories being last
to stubbornly fade away

Nothing's ever finished

What kind of magic is it
sticks us to each other
from encounter to lamination
a plywood of persons
subject to the weather
and the untested glue of love
then comes the fraying
and the parting of ways

Yet all it takes is a memory
of the red dress I bought you
that I never saw you wear
a dream of who we'd been

We are cities built atop each other
some collapsed completely over time
others in the process
still with pictures on the ruined walls
of times we can't forget
and wallpaper incompletely peeled
like nothing's ever finished
even though it has

Seeds

Love is not among the words we've spoken
but that's okay
perhaps it only waits to be said
like a thought waiting to be sprouted

Love should be a seed
soaked in time
and to grow if it will
and as flowers bloom from seeds
love can too

A word I would use now is thankful
for the time you chose to spend with me
for making me think of seeds
and flowers above all
thank you for making me think of flowers
for how else can seeds be made?

Sleeping in

Mountains move
(sliding under the mantle)
while the aftershocks subside slowly
hillocks and valleys floating
like swells above the rift

And I think about people sleeping
(sleeping together)
covered against the cold
creating planets while they dream
the continents drifting lazily
plates shift
below some warmer limb

We are the body
(a Big Bang Milky Way)
two suns mixing atoms
resulting in explosions
the earth moving as it must
and as we sleep the aftershocks
shake our sleeping forms

Mountains move
(like some snow-white quilt)
and in the avalanche
we touch under the mantle
then go on sleeping
as mountains are prone to do

Stayed the Night

Curled up next to me
snuggled in that human way
I listened to you sleep

I offered you rest
after what we stirred up
a random meeting's aftermath

And felt protective of your
each sleeping breath
I held you blossom
until we bloomed

Storms will come from this
I know
hold me in their wake

Summer's end

Warm covers pulled up tight
against the chill
waiting for the dawn
another day alone
like yesterday and tomorrow
where has the hope disappeared
fed by summer's promises
his dreams cold as an empty bed

He strains to remember her words
that she'd return to him soon
sealed with a kiss he could still taste
time had passed without a trace
except the sun grew dimmer
house and heart darkening in kind
he shivers now from the lonely bitter cold
and unreasonably blames
a season that has ended

The Footprint of the Snipe

Let us walk this bit
along the coast
where histories were created
where we have never walked before

It is new ancient surf
this palette of fresh sand
and new too the footprint of the snipe

The headland beckons
stretching all the way to China
between the rocks and whales

A river joins an ocean
where the beach runs south
we will not see the end
standing at its beginning

We are an empty beach
driftwood not yet recently washed ashore
a moon spreads out virgin sand
walk this bit with me

The Painting

I would like to show you
what appears to be a painting
of a plain and rough-hewn wooden table

The planks are smooth
though they have no paint or polish
and on the table is a vase

It is tall and made of clearest glass
full of water that seems to sparkle
as if freshly came from snow-melt streams

The vase is slender and quite simply made
and halfway up is tied a single ribbon
it is long and red and loosely fashioned
in a bow

A table with a red-ribboned vase
and in which sits a yellow rose
the color of the sun

Dale Brabb

Its stem as green as grass in spring
with two crisp leaves on either side
as if the rose were newly cut

This painting of a table and a rose
I don't think has a frame
and yet I see it where it hangs upon the wall
in the kitchen of my heart
I hung it there for you

The Queen's lace

Early morning road
taking me someplace else
burly June sun young in the sky
nearby hills wearing a misty veil

The Queen Anne's lace in full bloom
a cool breeze off the fields
sweeps the strong scent
through my open window
I have to stop

Like an invocation of herbs
the smell takes me down
dusty dirt roads of the past
when then it promised me
a blooming truck-garden of the heart

Lacy white doilies wafting
a red spot in the middle
marking the end of a queen's reign
and I sit stunned as if struck myself
by the edge of memory

Dale Brabb

A flock of chattering birds
fly across my vision
and I am back in the raucous present
blackbirds with red-flashed wings
intrude on my thought

Like fog lifted by a rising curtain of birds
I see the road ahead
and pulling away from old spells
once again I begin to travel
the highway of the deposed
breathing the fresh air of exile

The lost-wax process

The last time I got married
my new wife made me a wedding ring
incorporating my previous one
to make the symbol of eternity I desired
a snake swallowing its tail

It was beautiful my snake
with a tiny onyx eye
for my birthstone
and an ivory fang clasping the tail

She really was quite talented
and I probably should have kept it
but I'd lost the reason to
when it didn't mean what I'd took it for

Like eternity
only a lick and a promise
to be melted down later and recast
using the lost-wax process

The Playground

It all goes so much faster now
even the seeking of love
brings heart-break
hope tainted from the beginning

I heard the coyotes sing
when I was young
now I am filled with dread
to remember their wild song
in my bones and marrows

Love was so much simpler then
I didn't know my future would be tangled-up
in the mood-swings
or that depression rides joy
like a painted pony
in the playground

What if you came at last to me?

Would you bring your candlelight?
Your shadow dance and ancient eyes
your magic runes
and goddess' tunes
harvests borrowed from the moon?

And would I sing the rain for you?
And growing seeds
music from inside the stones
burrows deep in mountains steep
to safely carry us to sleep?

What should we call it if you did?
What words would fit
to cross that bridge
and would we know
the paths where lovers go?

And are the answers in the stars?
Are courses set
and prayers stockpiled
corners turned
and laughter earned
lessons finally learned?

Dale Brabb

What if you came at last to me?
Like destiny
or discovery
would that reveal
that what I feel
is not my imagination but real?

Who are you?

You who scribed across my heart
like ancient cave petroglyphs
emotional graffiti

You who have touched me
in places I don't touch myself
leaving me burning and exalted

You who are a stranger
and yet so connected
I am a rock embraced by roots

You whose voice warms me
banishing cold and shadows
in sunlight

You who writes poetry
arousing and satisfying
and more sensual than dream

Who are you
entering my heart
while I hold the door open

Whoever you are take my smile as your own
pleasure and tears yours too for the taking
for all the tomorrows granted us

Here is a basket of my fragments
add yours and let us weave a macramé
as decoration for when houses become home

Waiting for the nova

The observatory was closed to us non-scientists
but the sky was open
at nine thousand feet
the mountain's thin night air thick with stars

We sat on the grass
at the edge of this strange galaxy
all familiar constellations
lost in the dust of a billion suns

It made me see how far apart we'd drifted
I was one step away from the vast universe
and about to leave you behind
and all you wanted
was to stay on this little rock with Jesus

Words and Morning Afters

The sun shines through my curtain
cars and airplanes and goodbyes
all in the past

Here come the words
trying to arrange themselves
into poetries of love

Jealous words left out
playing second fiddle the next day
to a tune played all night

Give the words their due
let them paint their pictures
this morning they're all I have

Words have no sense of now
and even at their best divination
cannot navigate a course

But let them try
if they'll sustain these memories for me
I pray they get them right

Chapter Five

THE NATURAL WORLD

These are poems about encounters with the natural world. Some are my own encounters, some are hypothetical encounters.

A GLIMPSE OF HEAVEN

I read somewhere how the Kiowa used peyote
barebones
strip away the white tufts of strychnine
and eat one button at a time
which as you try to soften in your mouth
says very clearly it is not food
even the throat rebels
(because the flesh of god
is not something to eat easily)

A sip of water
and one dried apricot in between
(which I cannot eat to this day)
after about five buttons
the corners of the rooms softened
and I was led to go up to the overgrown cemetery
behind the house
where there were no corners

Where God was everywhere and everything
and I was nature too
a place where I finally belonged
this curious batch of genes and atoms
back among its own kind
not so much on the earth as of it
a glimpse of heaven
where all the little pieces fit

Airstream Heaven

"The force that through the green fuse drives
the flower, drives my green age"
—Dylan Thomas

Someday I'll come home to live
in the Rest Easy Estates Mobile Home Paradise
just up the river past
the Ben and Kay Dorris Memorial State Park
and boat launch

But for now I am a tumbleweed
the winds on the highway
blow me skittering and uprooted
sunlight flashing on my silver sides

Yet to settle my Airstream down
in the brown dirt of home
seams embedded and at last immobile
then maybe I could break out
and like a new uncertain sun-seeking plant
finally begin to grow.

An octopus reflects

I see that little green-back
is living under the rocks
at moray point
I should hunt him out
if not he'll get so big
he'll hunt me

I look up
where water disappears to light
I went there once and nearly drowned
nobody can breathe light
this world is perfect but for that
only bubble-breathers live up there

I prefer my cave
I see much safety in the dark
belly full of crab
surging with the tide
at one with God
as I reflect him to be

At the Watering Hole

The towels are on a chair next to the tub
and when the hot and steamy water is drawn
the cat leaps up to lay on them

I lie there bathing
while she rests sphinx-like atop the towels
watching

There is something eternal in her eyes
for a second I am an animal at the waterhole
and two green eyes stare unblinking
waiting for that moment of inattention

Evolution is a funny thing
I give her a level stare
across these turned tables
and work soap into a washcloth
with my upper hand

Canaries

Years ago I was building a boardwalk in Sitka
and using Alaskan Yellow Cedar for trim-work

An old native couple came by everyday
in spite of the posted bear warnings
and they were curious about my work
"What kind of wood is that?" they asked

Alaskan Yellow Cedar I told them
like all those trees up there on the hillside
the bare ones without needles

"Oh yes" the woman said
"The cedar people died a hundred years ago"
nobody knew why
an infestation of some kind of bug I'd guess
the trees no more than canaries in a coal mine

That happens a lot these days
only now we know why
our choice as citizens of the earth
is to try our best to combat that trend
or hold funerals for canaries
until we replace them on the pyre
we are building for ourselves

Close the window

The last night of August
I heard the frogs through my open window
or they might have been crickets
whatever

I was hearkened back
almost like
voices heard in the womb maybe

I shouldn't make too much of it
except this could be the last time
I hear it
the frogs are dying
crickets poisoned
and when I die my memories die too

Never mind
if you've trouble sleeping
just close the window
so nature can't intrude

Farming the wild blackberries

My hands are rough
and used to it by now
farming the wild blackberries
trying their best to grow up over the barn

Chopping out old canes in Spring
spurs the new ones to thrive
like pussy-willows sprouting on barbed wire

Then snowy blossoms to remind me
(scored later by cat-claw vines)
that a bloody harvest can be won
and then cobbler served with cream
thorny wines aging
and foolishly feeling some upper hand

While underground a plan grows
of the master bramble
roots like silent snakes
unobserved and unplanned
sneaking through the dirt

A war without end
a stand-off at best
between invasive species
there are no winners or losers
farming the wild blackberries

Dale Brabb

Fire-dancing

We swirled around the fire
dancing skin and hair all akimbo
laughing faces in and out of light
darkness finally won

Birds woke me in the tall grass
blinking eyes and fuzzy memory
the sun a blaring trumpet
clothes perfumed with ash

The fire-ring broken like an hourglass
sand melted into mirrors
insubstantially I rise to my feet
a plume of smoke between breezes

Free verse resume

Give me freedom and I'll choose
a string of images
every third one with a twist
because poets are mysterious
don't ask a man to rhyme
when he's too mysterious

I love the open range
with its bumps and vales
prairie dogs
a fringe of aspen on the edge
mesas sans toupee

I love it for one reason
eccentric paths
the busy rock avoiding green
seeing one-half the moon
behind the trees

And then the matter of the heart
shadows thrown on a wall
I am a poem that came to me one night
when repetition mated with condition
feelings do not pigeonhole
unique as chromosomes
love a snowflake melting on your tongue

Dale Brabb

So many ways to say truth
language ground down to sand
and heaped into dunes
joyful cries sweeping round the earth time after time
who teaches ears to hear?

Words pile on words
like a human jetty
a concrete affection
another freshet gushing from the wall
costumes donned and curtains pulled aside
and maybe drive-by wisdom
those are the elements of my resume

Onions

Last summer when my housemate went insane
she destroyed my garden of onions
batting them around the yard in the middle of the night
and I abandoned the ones she didn't find to their fate

The ones that she left were not deterred
and wintered over to sprout in the Spring
univerally splitting into halves

All the onions we eat are from that first batch
whole and hearty
sliced and diced to our heart's content
you never see twin onions at the supermarket

After a time the sprouts began to die off
but then flower stalks emerged
and they turned into tall blooming onions
those twin bulbs at the bottom providing nourishment

I marvel to see this happen
having always used the onion myopically
and never letting it reach its potential until now
will they make seeds to reseed their ruined bed?

Dale Brabb

It has been educational to live through this
sometimes what seems a setback isn't one at all
but rather a change of perspective
and though I've been eating adolescent onions my
    whole life
I can't imagine life without them

Jordan Lake Meditation

The lake is full of milt
salmon stacked up
waiting for culmination
trees bathe their feet
while a bear paces the far shoreline
in this jungle of the north
life and solitude
maintain an abundant balance

Paradise

Life is too tiny to be seen
and too large to understand
coils of ribbons in which we perceive
God's deliberate hand

Do amoebas dream of heaven
did Jesus die to save a tree
are we really any different
or just consumed with vanity

All life's composed identically
each double-helix the same
yet roses don't have a gene
for either sin or shame

Pride makes us think we're special
and has made us blind
like we're the most important thing
invented during Intelligent Design

Heaven is too random to be seen
too large for small minds to equal
making this paradise insufficient
while we're praying for the sequel

Still life

Unlit a candle rests
and waits for night
to burn with temporary life

The sunlit rose blazes brightly
until night
when petals drop one by one
like final tears

The poet's eye records the scene
in memory
where candles do not melt
and roses bloom until
eyelids fall like petals
to the darkness

The holly tree

I have a picture that I took
of a red-breasted sapsucker
perched on the trunk of a holly tree
with rows of his previous work
clearly evidenced

It had been a scraggly male holly
too close to the foundation
the landlord decreed
and now laid down in the yard
a four-foot stump all that was left

I was taking a break when he showed up
and perched on the stump
like he was thinking about making more holes
so I had time to get my camera
he's looking right at me taking his picture
maybe wondering why the tree's so short
I don't know

I've always had an interest in birds
know most of them by sight
and here I was reducing this bird's habitat
while also empathizing with him for his loss
a moment of interspecies communication
there at the holly tree
before I finished cutting it down

The half-life of forever

Circles will collapse in on themselves
their illusion is unnatural
for circles have no strength
beyond imagination
beyond the strength of lines
beyond the scribing compass' central point

Where zero is the ultimate round number
true patience can be only glimpsed sometimes
in matter
in ways we find unwelcoming
inscrutable to finite minds

We have not made the wheel conform to earth
but rather try to change the earth
and tame it to a mill
and by its tether lead it round and round
grinding out slow progress
in animation do we find the need
to count until the atoms come to rest

We do not see that time is malleable
and stiffly folded in our shrouds we wait
our bodies arrogant
our bodies falling back
into eternal dust

Ringing all our great bells
in the towers of belief
we create recurring echoes we call hours
that make a sound specific to our ears
and believing these waves we've set in motion
still keep on surging endlessly
until they break on heaven's shore
we tick off on our fingers
the half-life of forever
yet grieve to see the setting of the sun

Transient flowers

All day I stacked fresh white boards
coming down the chain belt
while strands of butterflies
like kite-tails cut loose
migrated north over the planer shed

I hoped they could travel far enough that day
following their ragged trail-blazing
to find standing trees somewhere
which like transient flowers
they'll bring to bloom

Trees

I used to look at trees from the viewpoint
of a man who heated his house by burning wood
is it good fuel?

Then I learned to prune
how to get the best fruit
and make the tree strong at the same time

So then I collected the fruit tree parings
and dried them as fuel for my barbeque

It is hard to escape my destiny of being a human
with its burden of family trees
we can't see the forest for all of them

I think we need to learn to live with the trees
stop clear-cutting the lungs of the earth
as a favor to those species who need to breathe Oxygen

Withering

Withering the stem
after the flower
leaves and all gone
where has vagrant Spring blown?

Well-chosen thorns escape the blade
worms return all to earth
why does my old love
back turned to me
keep bringing me where sepulchers bloom?

Withering appears to be a talent
I don't have
yet I'm meant to learn

Chapter Six

ODD GRANDPA

*As I've aged I've become more odd.
This chapter is a collection of miscellaneous
poems reflecting that.*

A great deal more

I am a pile of receipts
from the grocery store
stacked up to my present height
which has stabilized
since I earned enough to support myself
(I get a plastic card for my loyalty)

I supplement my diet
by growing food in my yard
you should too
and though it can never be enough
it is a great deal more
than I would have
by sitting on my hands

A Skylight

I opened up the closet door
put the bats and spiders on notice
no sense ignoring all that old stuff any longer
it'll be good to air it out
let whatever's in there catch it's breath
before it goes away

I need to make some room in there
maybe put in a skylight
to brighten the place up a bit
give all that baggage and old shoes
(I've walked my last mile in them)
to Saint Vinnies
just say goodbye to the past

It's not any kind of ritual
for sure not an annual event
but it seems the time has come
and though it might hurt a little
I hope I'll feel better after a while
a skylight might help

Dale Brabb

Acropolis

It's all crumbling now
that seat of wisdom
blue-veined marble facades
scored with the acid rain

When I was younger
temples were taller
philosophy an endless fountain
shaped in the form of Grecian deities

But even stone rots
everything has a half-life
and all the libraries
ultimately thrown into the bay
like overdue blocks

It's all crumbling now
look you've soiled yourself again
I can't help but wonder about my own future now
wandering unaware and lost
in the maze of my personal Acropolis

Baseball on the Radio

I remember listening to baseball on the radio
my mother and the World Series
entranced me at an early age
even out in the wastelands of Idaho
I will never understand her attraction to it
she wasn't at all athletic

Then as a young boy in Oregon
I listened to baseball on the same old Borg radio
extra-innings let me stay up
under the lights
vendors crying
"peanuts, cracker-jacks, ice-cold beer"
the sharp smack of the bat
my young voice adding to the swell of the crowd
as the ungoverned ball
bounced down the right-field line

Only later I learned
how the play-by-play
was proclaimed breathlessly
from a radio studio far from the game
a pencil hitting a microphone stand
my drive down the line
the same litany of refreshments
and crowd noise just a recording

But I didn't care
my imagination took me out to the ball-game
immersed in the statistics and drama
broken-hearted and exalted by turns
peanut shells and empty beer-cups scattered
about the bedroom floor of my memory

Anima

My shadow walks behind and ahead
an insubstantial proof
a transient blazing
to me a mystery
that part which will not die
an animation of the soul

Reflecting equal measures of dark and light
this fleeting replica of life
our hope for divinity extols
while outside of our control
nature pumps the blood
a metronome for angels and beasts alike
a concern to only those
casting viable shadows

After that is anyone's guess
so many trailheads advertised
so few pilgrims coming back with maps
so we keep composting our shadows
where they'll be safe
in the dirt that we know
while hoping they frolic
in some elsewhere

Apparent reasons

I fill the room with legal smoke
and don't that put paid to guilt
with its attendant paranoia?

(this is not a yelp review
for what anyone else should do)

A half century ago
I was in a station-wagon
somewhere outside of Bellingham
smoking the Mexican dope
and I was unsure of my "high"

We passed a road-sign
for a town called Sedro-Woolley
and I burst out laughing
for no apparent reason
that it still makes me laugh might just be
more information than you require

Borrowed dust

And a man grows as a mountain
snow-capped and piling
dreams to the sky
a new and vigorous volcano
full of hopes and visions
to change what the world offers
out there in the foothills

And then a man has to stand there
and the weathering starts
veils of dreams falling away
subjected to time's caustic wind
while the mountain pushes on within

It's then a man needs new hopes
or else fall down
then to count blessings
like a mountain should to the sun
every day its borrowed dust
casts another shadow

Dale Brabb

Broken Trail

Day after day me and the big Norwegian
tear up the rotten rain-soaked trail
armloads of wood roughly carried
up steep hillsides
hiding it so folks using our new trail
see nothing but the wilderness
he seems indestructible
while I stumble

Later around the campfire
we pass the pipe and drink deserved beer
he talks about the body breaking down
twenty years his senior
and already broken down
I advise him not to do this kind of work
when he's my age

Columbian cat and mouse

I didn't know the Spanish words
for spermicidal jelly
so I told them contracepcion
which raised their Catholic eyebrows
in that back room at the Cali airport
if amoebas had not tied my guts in knots
I would have laughed

They thought we'd been in Lima
so surely we had cocaine in our bags
with casual disdain they played with the mice
they'd caught
the usual mercy found in cats

After half an hour
they struck bonanza
mining the cosmetic bag
with patience I didn't feel
and red bananas I'd unwisely ate for breakfast
rolling warlike in my belly
I explained with all my available Spanish
about spermicidal jelly and Godless diaphragms

Disgusted they handed back the fruitless tube
no cocaine came out when they squeezed it
only slippery byproducts
of sins they couldn't share
so reluctantly they let us go
foreign contraception not against the law

"Where is the cat-box?"
I asked them in my broken Spanish
when they were finished
before remembering in my distress
the word for bathroom

Colorblind

I am white and I admit it
pale to the point of invisibility
but if Picasso painted me
and the light was good
I bet he'd find my color
mixing his paints
amid curses in Spanish

I can just see it now
a painting of me on a gallery wall
black lines in the rough shape of my face
(anatomy not being his strong suit)
but the color
me as spring perhaps
or a shade of winter
shimmering summer or umber autumn
some kind of color anyway

Then I wouldn't be so pale or invisible
he's Picasso after all and quite famous
accused of many things over the years
but not colorblindness
I'm sure he could make something out of me
and it's about time someone did

Dear Emily

Drinking coffee early Sunday morning
at the geezer bench
not fifty yards away in the meadow
people are losing the battle with gigantic bubbles
trying to keep them up

Emily leans against me and withholds judgment
she'd drifted in a few moments before
out on the path last night
she'd lost her ability to speak fluent sense
and really was far too young for the geezer bench any-
    ways
even on a Sunday morning
but there she was
and could only whisper
above the hubbub of the bubbles

"Lively up yourself" she breathed into my ear
 as the air escaped
dear Emily
collapsing on my shoulder
like a bubble you can't keep up

Elvis on mushrooms

My buddy's birthday was on Thanksgiving that year
so we feasted at his house before seeing Elvis
he had tickets for everybody
along with a handful of 'liberty caps'
he believed in "gifting" for his birthday

It was the old Elvis
not that it mattered
because I think once an Elvis
always an Elvis

I got to watch him wipe his famous brow
on a silk scarf hung round his neck
then nonchalantly whip it
into the mosh-pit of middle-aged birds
one lucky chick getting it
and scurrying away with her prize
while his stage toady
burdened with silk scarves
draped Elvis with another

Dale Brabb

It was a trip
his charisma still palpable
all the way to the sacred statement
after he'd finally gone
that "Elvis has left the building"
only then did it sink in it was over
and I had been party to a phenomenon
now struck off the bucket list
and something no one will ever see again

Butterfly wings

I've had dreams with that bare-beach thing
stretching way out there
exposing abandoned pools of anemones
which resulted in tsunamis
So tread carefully and don't throw pebbles into ponds
as the results can be tragic
and be careful too
when butterflies get the wind up

Don't wait up

As an older person I like to get mail
it turns out I'm a demographic
but that doesn't mean I need a reminder
about my freshness date
but thanks anyway
your letter helped keep things in focus

I have thought about internment
who wouldn't?
maybe a cedar tree planted on top of me
(probably not as good as a stone marker
in some long run
but I doubt it's worth my worry)

Cremation works for me
thank you for your interest
I'll get back to you
don't wait up

Expecting mercy

Why are we so afraid to share
like privileged children guarding a hoard of toys
streets of the world teem with hungry mouths
so we lock our doors
our private feast secure
voiding to help ourselves to more

A quirk of fate mixed these genes we carry
while without a shoe the other foot is bare
we flush more water than thirsty lips can drink
and make an industry of waste
inventing things that show we've lost the meaning
of the word "want"

When threatened we unleash expensive fury
and fill God's ears with prayers
our blessings to preserve
it's obvious our prayers are heard
just look around you

But we have every right to fear
since we have everything to lose
yet what kind of mercy should we expect
when we deny so many even that?

Dale Brabb

Gifts

Gifts are a curious blessing
to the gifted

I can put my hands on a person
(animal or human)
and my fingers know
the links of stiffness and pain
and what to do for release
it is a gift

When I tried to do it for money
I was left unsatisfied
as if using my gift that way
was not its purpose
so now I do not advertise

And if I put these hands on you
it is because I want to
because you are worth it
(animal or human)
and we will both secrete hormones
of pleasure
which is the nature of giving and receiving gifts

I am no longer silent

I do not write for you
who never heard my words
deafened by
fossilized teeth

I do not write little puzzle books
and third dimension games
for head-scratching fellows
writing grants

I do not etch cemetery stone
in praise of my betters
but write of the living world
and footsteps to follow today

These words will not reverberate
in your circle
but it is no matter
my poetry's not meant for you

Dale Brabb

In the light of stars

Yarrow stalks lie scattered like soda straws
fate's arrow spinning round the dial
randomly pointing in all the directions toward eternity

My karma is at cross purposes
coins dumbly charting hexagrams
I disregard the flow
blood just a map beneath skin

Some oracles spoke from lips of gods
accounting puzzled mazes
but I cannot even see my shadow
the stars have grown too dim

Haphazardly I pick up sticks
and two-faced luck
I need to keep the feet walking
as if my mind was made up
my shadow playing tag
until it too deserts me

Welcome to the mirage

A lizard in the doorway seems to sleep
with one eye closed
when I pass a tongue tastes the air

Las Vegas is a subterfuge by day
all light and mirrors at night
where you pay for smiles
people follow the Goodyear trail
wearing juke-box masks
the smell of old meat turning slowly
on a one-armed barbeque
a museum ran by enablers

Car-horns drive the streets weaving through drunks
shell-game middens pile the clod-hoppers dirt
while desperation licks its lips
glad to be home
knowing you brought something
why else are you here?

Later a song about love whispers
through an automatic door
like a salve
a memory of a better somewhere
played to quiet the unquieted soul
until like everyone else passing by
it's gone

The lizard seems to sleep
its tongue tracing empty forms
on doorways left behind
but he isn't worried
sooner or later sustenance comes
the mirage brings it in

Invitados only

I'm with Pignatoro
a tanner born a tanner's son
brash and bold and of Italian descent
almost rich
with a muscle car
and a condo in the outskirts of Callao
where the old rich go for Carnival
he thinks my white American nobility
will get him in the door
at a party of his betters
right down by the shore

Their courteous rejection
is as gentile as my apology
of course I understand
it is a party for invitados only

We walk away
and he swears blackly at the blue bloods
his burly peasant shoulders
bunched like fists
I smile serenely
half-believing they'd have let me in
but for this surly tanner's get
I nod at passers by
almost a gentleman
while beside me like an angry Etna
the Pignatoro fumes

Dale Brabb

McDonald Lake

I remember a picture
the lake at twilight
a northern sun set incompletely
one bald-eagle flies across chittering

We sit feeding spruce to the little fire
a chill on a summer's night
bugs finally resting
beer-cans crushed
the cedar people a hundred years dead
glow phosphorescent behind the lake

We douse the fire and then look up
over the lake an aurora borealis has spread
a blue-green scarf across the sky
exposing my memory like a photograph

Miranda's hat

Ah to feel the blessings
the fecund earth out dancing
casabas bouncing on the vine
the mating sun and moon

So goes this simple life
all amplitude and harvest
glories of the fertile flesh
promissory pips and pits

There are no whores in nature
no sandwich signs or neon
just yeast and naked dreams
clothed in genetic skin

Our brains turn our heads
but the core is organic
and in the moment when the music stops
we pile into Miranda's hat

Of Zen and irony

The Transcendental Meditation master
in the middle of most Catholic Peru
explains the hazards he's encountered
to his peaceful equanimity
as he skillfully prepares cocaine

Sent out from his native Spain
he had expected hardships
to be more spiritual in nature
quoting Oscar Wilde in his lisping Castellano
(the perfect gay man's language
he laughingly admits as he outs himself)
"puedo resistir todos excluyendo temptacion"*
it is a mantra
full of Zen and irony
none of us can resist repeating

* "I can resist everything except temptation"

Passage

I've slept in houses built by pioneers
in the night limbs blew down
from giant oaks those pioneers planted
the West was close that night

Indeed the West is just below the tarmac
the part not modern
rocks too hard and too many to break up
water un-stopped
on its way to the Western sea
whirlwinds dancing in the desert
fire crowning through treetops

The West is also things we couldn't use
weeds growing through the litter of farm machinery
around abandoned homesteads
tumbleweeds piled up on fences
a pile of mule-deer scat
wild songs from the rim-rock

True West is there forever
though ice covered it thousands of years
to come again as it wills
a higher power foreclosing on our deeds here
and one who surely won't mourn our passage

Phases

As a moonchild
I am used to all those
comings and goings
eclipses and their varieties

The moon releases the romantic
when it's full anyway
but nobody heralds
the "Blood-red strawberry new moon"
and half-moons get little press
while lesser phases are relegated to finger-nails
if noticed at all

To me that moon is always there
no matter the illumination
if I stood on its surface looking at our earth
wouldn't I see us going through the same phases?

A moonchild has a broader perspective
more attuned to the larger universe
and so I can see that dark side of my own planet
is just a phase it's going through

Poetry

It's like sculpture
though I don't need that big of a room
they're still standing there displayed
all my brave poems
I can whack a piece off where it's needed
digitally

Except
I also can add things
creation goes both ways
what a hoot
glad I'm cast in God's image
creationwise I guess
even when the things I don't believe
will send me straight to hell

Dale Brabb

Possession

I've been told there is a god-shaped hole
a universal vacuum in our souls
we try to fill with drugs or sex or deities
believing we are incomplete

And so I tasked my will to dig
a hole where one did not exist
then a hunger raged through me
and ravenous I ate the world
gorged myself on appetizing heavens
swallowed angels whole and looked for more

When I was done with gluttony
I filled the hole back in
for the good of all
and pledged to never be possessed
by spirits not my own

Privilege

Have you never been hungry
I mean really hungry
have you never been cold
with no way to get warm
have you never needed sleep
and had no place to lay your head
then you are privileged

It isn't your fault
merely a quirk of fate
but that doesn't absolve you
from willful blindness
your luck does not confer superiority
privilege is just another hurdle
(if you want to be worthwhile)
to get over

Dale Brabb

RIGOLETTO

I gifted him a framed picture of Rigoletto
when he moved in
a welcome-wagon kind of thing
a man seeking quiet and solitude
choosing a clown from my gallery of frames
but then he was writing his novel
right next door in the quiet
I heard his typewriter banging away
so go figure

When he moved out he took Rigoletto
which was his to keep
leaving a dirty blender and some other crap
out on the parking by the street
a broken bookcase
a folding TV dinner tray
an office chair that tempted me
I am a sucker for ergonomics

How can we understand artists?
leaving behind cleaning supplies
on a bench in the foyer
like they'll never need them again
and six cans of assorted
organic beans
like there's no tomorrow
and yet taking the Rigoletto

Ruby

Where is our Ruby?
she is sleeping in the river
stones are her pillows
the current plays with her
an arm goes gently up and down
like she's waving

Ruby lost her arms up to the elbow
in the train-yard
passed out when she was drunk
a railcar pinched them off
she surprised the sacred sisters
when she lived through that

Be nice to Ruby
throw some change in the pouch
she got at Goodwill
her whole life's in there
and look the other way
when she talks to spaces in the air
yet no matter how she pleads
the silent angels scream at her

Dale Brabb

Be nice to her
and she'll lead you to the liquor store
please reach right in her pouch
enough panhandled money for a pint
then pour it in the cup she found at Circle-K
and she'll smile around the flexy straw
that secret smile
and clap her phantom hands

Ruby lived on the mall
beloved in a way
to the circle of revolving folks
loud and rough as fighting crows
spare-change hands to feed her scraps
a dirty sleeping bag at night
hiding from the sweeping cops
almost a kind of safety

By the river in the night
someone tipped the bottle and she drank
beneath the bridge the dirty beach
no eyes saw what happened next
the darkness was complete
perhaps she fell when she was drunk
passed out again
the river runs to rapids there

Where is our Ruby
who was somebody's child one time
where did that girl go?
she slipped unseen into the night
and wasn't missed for several days
the angels screaming in her head
are silent now

Look at her sleeping where the current plays
beyond haphazard charity at last
beyond the broken bottle ghosts
and dreamlike does her empty arm
go slowly up and down
as if she waves goodbye

Salient moments

Promise me a word
when I might need it
like a lighthouse
to find my way to port
that time when changes
come upon me unawares

Promise me you'll notify my next of kin
identify my tattoos
and generic genetic flaws
like ears hanging out
or my lack of fashion sense
something
since I might wash up unidentified

Because I'm like to lose it now
cast into some alien constellation
never to be seen again hereabouts
but on a clear night
and I might need that lighthouse light
to find my way back

It would have to be tomorrow
'cause now I'm captured in a web
of stars and salient moments
adrift in a larger cause
and who knows when it will end
all I'm asking is keep a watch
in case it does

Since

I remember that time you kissed me in public
you wanted all my geezer friends
sitting on the bench behind me
to be envious
and they were!
being kissed like that by a young woman
a thing dreams are made of

Of course it was no big thing
just part of the flow of that day
and I am surprised to even remember it
except for the fact
I ain't been kissed like that since

Roofing

They are stripping the roofing off the house across
    the street
I've done that before

I remember stripping the roofing off maybe six covered
    bridges
straddling streams and creeks
even some major rivers

These guys are lucky
if they fall off
at least they won't get carried downstream very far

The Failed Intervention

She walked along the river Cauca
in a park in Cali, Colombia
carrying two empty cans of paint
and arguing loudly
with people not there

Splashing river water into a can
(once filled with silver paint)
she stirred it with her hand
shouting at the same time
and pointing a silver finger
at one invisible chastising person
after another

Done mixing she drank it off all
silver paint and river water
and walked away upstream
against the current
still carrying both cans
another failed intervention left behind

The Highest Accolade

The highest accolade a human can achieve
is to be someone
others want to know better
and when you go you don't leave a hole
where you were
but a hole still full of you
words and actions
and the half-life of love
which can take forever to dissipate

The Museo de Oro

The Museo de Oro in Cuzco
is filled with the memory of gold
down the street
a shop sells Alpaca sweaters
where the boy tending the shop
offered me a 'pre-Columbian' antiquity
complete with guilty glances up and down the street
it was a lion's head cast in brass
red paint scraped away
to show me the 'oro'
I tell him I am shopping for sweaters
but I get a chilly thrill
like a smuggler must feel
and though there were no lions in Pre-Columbian Peru
I came back again the next day

But the shop was closed
sealed shut by two heavy wooden doors
studded with painted lion's heads
a gap here and there I'm sure
as a result of the market in antiquities

The myth of purity

We've done better with dogs and cats
and thorougbred cattle
but as for humans
we've lost the context
as soon as Cro Magnon
mated with Neanderthals and Denisions
we lost thoroughbred status
and became a mixed species of races

And it didn't stop then
when KKK members do their DNA
they find facts in the woodpile
that sullies their narrative of "white" purity
and all manner of interbreeding with "subhumans"

Religion hasn't helped
our gods are not pure either
angels mating with young girls to produce a savior
bulls covering swans shouldn't be surprising
since we invented gods in our own impure image

Yet we are pure humans
and capable of reproducing the animal flawlessly
with all of our warts and freckles intact
but nothing has proved more pernicious
to humans living on this planet
than the myth of purity

The Pioneer Bar

I stand shoulder to shoulder
with my fellow frontiersmen
at the Pioneer Bar in Sitka
on mainstreet if you can find that
lining the walls are photographs
fishing boats stranded on rocks
tilted impossibly
like my fellows at the bar
waiting for the fucking tide
that lifts us off this rock

Dale Brabb

Utopia

In my town ancient single people
walk their ancient pets
collecting the refuse
as they go
proud to recycle

Such actions confuse the dogs
but that's another matter

I can't think how utopia
could be much better
everyone a rescue animal

But then again I'm a socialist

Walls

A thousand years ago
the king of this island was deposed
and abandoned his castle walls

I am just among the latest conquerors
of this people
and looking down at the busy neon street
full of opportunities below
I sit basking in the moonlight
resting my back for a moment
on an abandoned wall
over a thousand years old

Welcome to my world

The fly sat there all day
listening to the screen-door
banging on an occasional hinge

Very slowly the sun climbed up
the faded yellow wall-paper
until the shadows disappeared

The fly sat there anyway
as if with no place else to go
so hot its wings were sweating

The curtains looked out in the street
though there's not much to see there
the eye not drawn to so much nothing

Welcome to my world
wipe your feet and set a spell
I could do with the company

What's for Lunch?

"Comedy is the crazy stuff in my life
that would be funny
if it were happening to someone else." (Richard Leebrick)

In "Much Ado about Nothing"
an old man in a wheelchair during the matinee
aroused himself from a nap
in the middle of my monologue as Dogberry the constable
asking in a loud voice
"What's for lunch?"

Life on stage is like a skating rink
either you got the style to keep skating
or you crash into the wall
and break your legs
like your well-meaning friends
implored you'd do

As it seems to fit

My old boss at the cannery
was a little guy
who'd spent years in submarines
back when he was in the Navy
and Frank used to say
"Christ in a teacup!"
when vexed

I didn't ask him what he meant by it
but find I use the phrase myself
now and again like he did
as it seems to fit

When the Titan shrugs

The mammoth stood serenely
in a prehistoric meadow
munching a mouthful of fresh hay
when the axis of the earth shifted
and a blast of frozen air
traveling thousands of miles an hour
froze him solid in thirty seconds

If a compass were invented
it'd have spun in circles madly
looking for magnetic north
which turned out hard to find
with up becoming down
left turning right
vice and versa topsy-turvy

What good will our inventions do us
when the titan shrugs again
will a deity step up to save us
those gods we hope exist
outside of science and triangulation

No god cries tears
when the earth changes course
no elephants were harmed in this poetry
the seeds of hasty unsaid prayers
are caught in our frozen mouths

Wise

Maybe I hadn't meant to be wise
when I got older
it just happened over time
when I wasn't looking
maybe in spite of baser actions
from my youth

But wise people don't brag about it
claim wisdom and you mark yourself
as still having a lot to learn
and you don't learn wisdom
can't buy it either
if it shows up act surprised
maybe no one will notice your insincerity

Wish me luck

I don't believe in God
and yet I blame Him anyway
for this pestilence of religions

And I really wish I could believe
it would make things so much easier
except for the grey areas
everything would be black and white
I'd be able to collect sins in a box
for recycling at Saint Vinnies
or spin prayers on the wind

But no I am bereft of praise
even amid this google of gospels
God's compass pointing everywhere
so I guess I'm on my own
just me and the earth
God has supposedly supplied for my use
trying to save it from His followers
wish me luck

Dale Brabb

Chapter Seven

THE FUNNY PAPERS

I learned about satire at an early age reading MAD Magazine. These poems are what I used to call Bad Poetry, almost like cartoons, I hope the reader finds them amusing.

Caterpillar in denial

I am not a caterpillar, oh no!
perhaps you've misconstrued my shape
you think
millipede or those horrible
ninjas of the nature world
the centipede
no I am none of those
I'm not a caterpillar
first of all

I'm not a flutterby
I'm no Mothra
queen of molts
or even a paltry larva
leave me be

no caterpillar
no leaf-chewer
no cocoon weaver
no green-horn

Dale Brabb

so let me out the jar
let me crawl
to fly
to transmogrify
I am not a caterpillar
oh no!!

oh you little excrement
with your beastly
Far Side collector's jar
let me out you cull
I am not the bug you seek
you changeless
boring get

Eye am camera

I snap you up
another one standing in front of the fountain
like a gnome by any other name
I am the same

You are mind now
filmy as perceived
a face peering into the porthole
I click you

It is to travel in my re-memory
my card and chip
my f-ing stop
light meters ahead of you
and zooming lens

You hang around my neck
bumping my exotic belly
until we next make port
safe inside my chuckle
I develop you

Don't ask me to promise
you could have been al fresco
a motionless statuary
or a birds-eye view

But I have you now
in my dark room
I bathe you
enlarging

Your mouth was open
your life stilled
art is not my middle name
eye am camera

Gardening priorities

You might think that gardens are for swells
where prissy flowers grow just for the smells
where bushes are cut in the shape of llamas
by someone hired by high class Mamas
"Right here I'd like a wall built out of shale
I'd help, but I'm afraid I'd break a nail!"
if I were judging gardens I would rate her
by her success at growing the potater

I cry to see the damages and evils
of Satan's minions, the potato weevils
and I recoil with horror and with fright
to think my fragile spuds could get the blight
you can have kohlrabi, fava beans and such
those crops don't interest me too much
but if to my attention you would cater
forget the rest and show me your potater

And elbow deep I'll search exotic muds
gently groping for reclusive spuds
some are juicy sweet and red, oh boy
some are bigger than my head, oh joy
and if you're smart you won't forget the fact
they'll be embraced by your digestive tract
Grandma was hale and hearty when she ate her
delicious daily rations of potater

So if you think that gardening just means
those pictures in the Sunset magazines
I'd advise you set your goals much higher
than those useless ornamentals you desire
or those tony vegetables that are so faddish
(radicchio is just a fancy name for radish)
if your garden is to be a pride inflator
get rid of all the plants that ain't potater

How do I love thee?

(Original by Elizabeth Barrett Browning)

How do I love thee? Let me count the ways.
I love thee to the depth and breadth and height
My soul can reach, when feeling out of sight
For the ends of Being and ideal Grace.
I love thee to the level of everyday's
Most quiet need, by sun and candle light.
I love thee freely, as men strive for Right;
I love thee purely, as they turn from Praise.
I love thee with the passion put to use
In my old griefs, and with my childhood's faith.
I love thee with a love I seemed to lose
With my lost saints—I love thee with the breath,
Smiles, tears, of all my life!—and, if God choose,
I shall but love thee better after death.

How do I love tree?

How do I love tree? Let me count the rings
I love tree to the girth, diameter and height
my chainsaw reach, a top that's out of sight
for board-feet and the cash it brings
I love tree to the level where it fell
financial need, by sun or truck headlight
I love tree freely, it is mine by rights
I love tree purely for the log to sell
I love tree when the winch is put to use
on my own truck, the first of many loads
I've loved tree since I did a timber cruise
with ancient maps—I love trees close to roads
tires, beers, my redneck life—and if Mills choose
I shall but love tree better when it's sold

Huevos Toreros

It happened once in Monterrey
a tourist stopped to break his fast
he stepped into a side café
hoping for some choice repast

He'd come there just the other day
huevos toreros on the sign
"Scrambled eggs and something, hey
that's how I want to dine"

He saw what they had served Jose
who sat behind a heaping plate
"Give me some too, without delay",
but found out he would have to wait

Jose had got the special
he alone would have some fun
what really makes it special?
each day they serve but one

But now it was the tourist's day
at the table soon to eat
anticipating that rich display
the glory of his special treat

Dale Brabb

Now came the waiter with a tray
the tourist clutching fork and knife
twice the cost he'd gladly pay
for one good breakfast in his life

At last huevos toreros on the table lay
one tiny plate could hold it all.
The tourist said with some dismay
"But wait, Jose's was not this small…"

"Senor you got the Special"
 as the waiter turned to run
"today its not that special,
 since last night the el toro won"

Leda and the Swan

(by W. B. Yeats)

A sudden blow, the great wings beating still
Above the staggering girl, her thighs caressed
By the dark webs, her nape caught in his bill,
He holds her helpless breast upon his breast.

How can those terrified vague fingers push
The feathered glory from her loosening thighs?
And how can body, laid in that white rush,
But feel the strange heart beating where it lies?

A shudder in the loins engenders there
The broken wall, the burning roof and tower
And Agamemnon dead. Being so caught up,
So mastered by the brute blood of the air,
Did she put on his knowledge with his power
Before the indifferent beak could let her drop?

Lexus and the semi

A sudden crash, the big tires turning still
above the wrinkled hood, airbags released
through seatbelt webs, a massive shiny grill
I am held helpless, glad the car is leased

How can the jaws of life so vainly pull
the steering wheel from my upholstered thighs?
and how can semi trailer loaded full
but fill the only space before my eyes?

A shudder as we two uncouple there
the Lexus crushed, the trucker is dismayed
and eighteen wheeler dead. Being thunderstruck
too flustered yet to pluck glass from my hair
did I make sure all premiums were paid
before my car was totaled by this truck?

Literary relaxative

O blessed forms from whence such meaty viands sprang
full-formed, like Agatha from the Zooster's head
half-glassed the stopper's op'd, verses beckon from the
    beaky brim
o'erfilled!! Stanza side and dribs and drablets on the tablet

those yoreful days gang aft the peaty poetist proclaimed
turgid flood running off the loch-fed pen, in the
    darkening ink
the fluted cork blown like wind-flossed bark, purging
    inspiration
released, my long and supple bottleneck, look out ye
    Gods!!

fraught with thought like fledgy warm reptiles floating
my mind's-eye sky spotted by imaginary migration
could I balk and thereby bilk, destined to the destination
    of my destiny
forbid the vulcanization remitting from my pregnant
    shell-incrusted headland?

Dale Brabb

deserve, observe, I serve, reversing enervation preserved
exhaling the spirits, dutiful conduit conducting, words
    like hoary seeds
spewing wizened wafting wisdom, wondrous as it
    was awaited
for too long have these fingers grown of quietude

O hear the ages calling, the time-vine fruit lades the tree
rictis flees! Once more effable fables fantastically flourish
un-penned, the pen pensively propels prodigious prolixity
un-stoned, Lazarus-like, Poetry arises lively from its
    gravid demise!

Hark Hornitos

*(sung roughly to the tune of
Hark the Herald Angels sing)*

Hark! Hornitos in a shot glass
glory to the Baja king!
Lupe fry me rojo snapper
Gringos can't cook anything
thank you to Social Security
a check like magic in the bank
I can't afford to live in Fresno
I was born at sixty-five
Hornitos makes my blood-work thrive

Generic drugs, you can't avoid them
apothecary on parade!
online, offline, it's no matter
Gringos will buy anything
in the sunset I am happy
in the sunset I will thrive
Hornitos if my Lupe serves it
Hornitos if I drink with somebody
Hornitos if I drink alone

Losing it, a Villanelle

Down the drain I go in tiny little strands
where is my vim, my vinegar, my morning wood?
I've forgotten all my well-laid plans

In youth my hair was thick, a full and healthy stand
but bareness grows where once a forest stood
and down the drain I go, in tiny little strands

Somewhere I've lost some urges from my glands
a lessened randy foolishness is good
and I've forgotten all my well-laid plans

My arms too short to see my hands
ears that hear less than they should
down the drain I go, in tiny little strands

I vowed I'd be Adonis striding through the lands
but now the only exercise I get is chewing food
I've forgotten all my well-laid plans

My shrunken-headed memory allows no demands
and no reason to remember, even if I could
down the drain I go, in tiny little strands
forgetting all my well-laid plans

Doc's Ode

A cursory examination shows
skin as white as a porcelain laving bowl
features that are too fine and delicate
for your standard Dwarfish taste
musculature not suited for working in the mines
and yet appealing in a most disturbing way

She appears to be unnaturally tall
with slender feet and shapely little toes
and matching hands whose long smooth fingers
will never properly grasp
the handles of our rough, coarse, grubbing tools

After much review
I have decided that cross-breeding with the subject
would not improve
the perfection of the Dwarf-like form

Sigh!!!

Perhaps I could convince her
that a more thorough examination
would not be out of order

Dale Brabb

Marie

Marie, Marie, I glow for you
from the inside out
can you not see me glowing?

I brought the stones to you
putting them in your indifferent pockets
piling them like crushed Stonehenges on your porch
bismuth, feldspar, the dangerous ores of love

your heat attracts me now
I cannot shield myself from your eyes
my life is measured in half-loves
inexorable, growing like pale lichen
on a moonless night

my disease clicks madly
bright machines do not wash it away
I dream I lay dreaming
in water too heavy for my skin
I am drained and plumbed
a tablet scored deeply by desire

Marie, Marie, there is no cure for this love
and from the inside out
I am glowing

Milking Time

The kitten has a white mustache
three squirts in the pail
pink tongue whipping like a lash
cats gather without fail

Three squirts in the pail
warm milk flowing faster now
cats gather without fail
quiet words calm nervous cow

Warm milk flowing faster now
twice a day I pull the teats
quiet words calm nervous cow
calf cannot restrain his bleats

Twice a day I pull the teats
Bessie's milk feeds all the farm
calf cannot restrain his bleats
so universal is milk's charm

Bessie's milk feeds all the farm
pink tongue whipping like a lash
so universal is milk's charm
the kitten has a white moustache

Dale Brabb

Mounting a la Natural

Even if they've a headache
Mrs Horny Toads feel compelled
to live up to their namesake

And black widow bachelors would do well
to be like coyote lovers
if in genetic spreading they'd excel

Studly dragon-flies don't need no covers
if tail-to-tail they'd mate
"Hey good looking, set your butt to 'hovers'!"

In watery caves eyeless fishes lie in wait
extinction drawing closer for their kinds
since blind boffing's elemental to their fate

In nature evolution furthers many lines
providing cornucopias of ways to poke behinds

Eleven-year-old in love

My love is like a bird
though not because she flaps around
or anything
but more like how when
I think of her
these thoughts perch on my brain
like a statue in the park

And that's not it either
my love is maybe like a rock
though not just any ordinary rock
oh no
a rock that's pretty inside
but then again how would you find
it's pretty inside unless you broke it?
and then my love would be like gravel

No, my love is like a cloud, that's it
her tears are like the rain
which is kind of sad
but she's also a happy cloud
a funny jokester cloud
and I'm going, "Hey that's not funny
quit blocking the sun!"
and then she spits water on me

Dale Brabb

Rupert's dream

I can't stand Barry Manilow, he writes songs that I abhor
his fans are sheep who think he's deep and loudly bleat
    for more
but up there in the spotlight, "Mandy" trilling like a flute
my fingers rush and buttons push to make the sucker mute

You'd think with all his sniveling, Barry's folks had
    named him Neil
for Diamond's sap and Sedaka's pap made that name
    non-pareil
Neil Young is an exception, though he's been known
    to whine
he caterwauls with bigger balls than all other Neils
    combined

I guess I never had a chance if I had hoped for fame
how could I top the charts of pop with Rupert for a name?
though I'll never get a Grammy, that's not my real
    complaint
my secret dream's to hear girls scream "Oh, Rupert" 'til
    they faint

Silent farts, horrid farts

(sung to the tune of Silent Night)

Silent farts, horrid farts
it wasn't me, it must be Mark
around the greenroom
air-freshener was sprayed
but the threat wasn't over
just merely delayed
it smells like bratwurst and peas
mustard and bratwurst and peas

Silent farts, horrid farts
stink-meter registers off the charts
Sam and Bill Wilcox
have innocent smiles
the pair of them squirm
like they're troubled with piles
somebody open the door
for God's sake please open the door

Silent farts, horrid farts
a quiet hiss as butt-cheeks part
radiance beams
upon Katya's face
people are fainting
all over the place
the air's turned green from the gas
revenge is now Katya's at last

The first John Deere

(sung to the tune of "The first Noel")

The first John Deere my Grandpa did buy
didn't smell like a mule but he gave it a try
didn't smell like a mule but it worked twice as hard
and in less than five minutes he plowed his front yard
John Deere, John Deere, John Deere, John Deere
that is the tractor we use around here

So Jimmy Bob (and Rufus too!) proudly brag without fear
that there's no tractor made can stand up to John Deere
when it comes to bottomland or stump-pulling too
if you aint got John Deere then you must be a fool
John Deere, John Deere, John Deere, John Deeeeerrrrree
that is the tractor we use around here

The gyro*

(A modern sonnet)

The skirt's high-heels and fishnets filled with gams
made me 86 my stakeout sweet and toot
a wolf like me just can't resist the lambs
my wing-tipped dogs set out in hot pursuit

I caught up with the shapely red-head moll
and pitched my voice down low like Barry White
"My life is incomplete without you, Doll
come paint the town with me some Friday night"

She turned to me and shot me down in flames
"Explain to me why you are not in class!"
I'm just a slave to dominating dames
surrendering my heart and forged hall pass

A fool I am, but more fool not to try
I'm gyroboy the teenage private eye

*slang term meaning beginner

The Virgil of the Colonel and the Bull

Oh come and sit beside me Cabbage Patch of genes
and I'll corral-alate my Virgil of the Colonel and the Bull

The mongrel sun sat bale and bleak
we'd only heard one brandy rooster craw
the Colonel clenched his hurly tools
to castigate the bollocks of the Bull

The Bull then gleaned the frosty news
of the Colonel's grimy tented mien
his tromboned horn flew up the scale
he prawned the dearth with ravage greed
and hotter than a jalapeno fence
he clanged the grate to flee to farts unknown

The Colonel reaped into his wrath
and broke the bread-long hoofy verge
the Bully cringed the Colonel hawed
"You burger-brain, you hay-lip drool!"
the Colonel's sward grew from his ham
and to throstleberries dipped and docked

An oyster here an oyster there sprinkled the llano
and to this day my pumpkin pearl
that Bull still sings soprano

You are abhorrent

(A sonnet to dysfunction)

You are abhorrent to my wand'ring eye
your touch I'm always eager to avoid
your sour breath will warn me that you're nigh
your voice does pain me more than hemorrhoids

Sweet flowers wilt beside the path you walk
your raiment Goodwill couldn't give away
the dogs of town do howl to hear you talk
at parties people leave if you would stay

I should prefer another planet's air
though I might choke when I do take a breath
rather than your oxygen to share
could I but choose then gladly I'd choose death

I wonder why I married you of course
and wonder more why you filed for divorce

Dale Brabb

ABOUT THE AUTHOR

I have been writing poetry for fifty years. It has always been a way for me to express thoughts and feelings, and most of the poems in this book are reflective of that. In the last ten or so years I've adopted a style with very little punctuation and using language that is easily understood.

www.ingramcontent.com/pod-product-compliance
Lightning Source LLC
LaVergne TN
LVHW012100070526
838200LV00074BA/3820